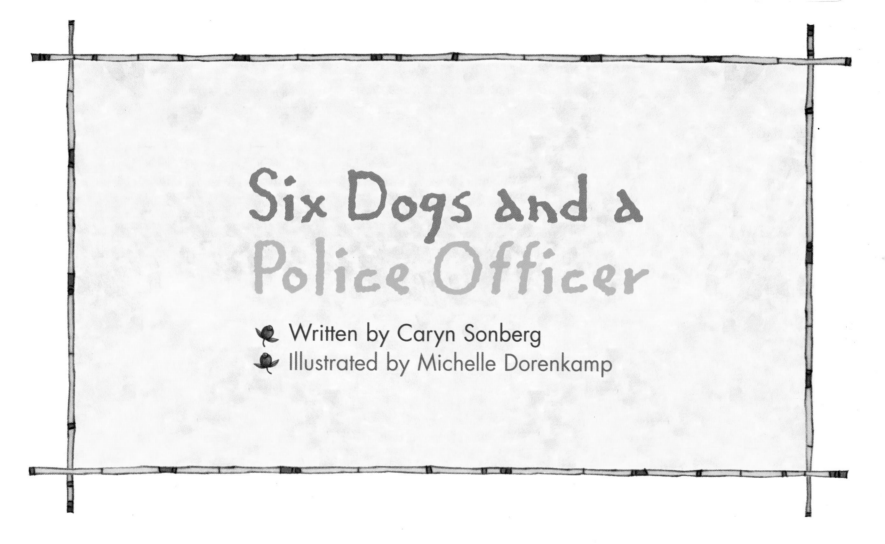

Six Dogs and a Police Officer

Written by Caryn Sonberg

Illustrated by Michelle Dorenkamp

Dedicated to my sisters, Patrice and Niki, for their love and support and for helping me find my way in life.
Caryn Sonberg

For Sweet Pea, with love—Mimi.
Michelle Dorenkamp

Ballard Tighe &

Copyright ©2005 Ballard & Tighe, Publishers, a division of Educational IDEAS, Inc. All rights reserved. No part of this publication may be reproduced in whole or in part, or stored in a retrieval system, or transmitted in any form or by any means, electronic or mechanical, including photocopy, recording, or otherwise, without permission in writing from the publisher.

2005 Printing • Cat. #2-374 • ISBN 1-55501-776-2

Editor
Dr. Roberta Stathis

Art Direction and Design
Danielle Arreola

Editorial Staff
Patrice Gotsch, Kristin Belsher, Linda Mammano, Rebecca Ratnam, Nina Chun

H ave a wonderful weekend ... and don't forget to read!" Miss Millie called out as the students packed up their belongings and began to file out of the classroom.

Miss Millie smiled at each student. Olive was the last one out. Miss Millie gave her the biggest smile of all.

3

STONEBRIDGE ELEMENTARY SCHOOL
Where Learning Is a Lifestyle

Olive looked at the enormous brown door and the sign above it that read: STONEBRIDGE ELEMENTARY SCHOOL: *Where Learning Is a Lifestyle.* Olive wasn't quite sure what that meant, but she read it every day as she left school.

Olive hurried to catch the school bus. However, just as she was about to climb aboard and give Mr. Beckett a big hello, she saw her mom across the street. "What's going on?" Olive shouted.

Olive's mom held out her hand as she reached Olive. "Take my hand, Sweetie. We have to cross the street to get back to the car."

"But, Mom, what are you doing here?" Olive asked.

"Well, Olive, your father and I have a surprise for you and your brother."

"We got a dog? Did we, Mom?
Did you get us a dog?" Olive asked.

"No, Olive, we didn't get you a dog,"
her mother replied. "Get in the car next
to your brother and I'll explain."

"This is better than a dog. It's an adventure!" Olive's mom exclaimed. "We packed all our bags and Mr. Malverne is picking up our newspaper. We're on our way to the city! We're going to take a vacation this weekend."

"The city?" Olive and Oliver asked at the same time. They didn't seem at all convinced that a visit to the city would be better than a dog. "What are we going to do in the city?" asked Olive.

"Oh, there is so much to do in the city," Olive's dad replied. "We can go to some museums, we can see a play, maybe do some shopping, and take lots of pictures of the tall buildings."

Olive rolled her eyes. Oliver stuck out his tongue and pretended to be throwing up.

"I see you two," Olive's dad scolded gently. He smiled his big, broad smile and said, "Trust me. You'll like the city."

Olive was unconvinced. "Why can't we go to Game World?
Or the water park? Or even to Grandma and Grandpa's?"

"Don't worry, Olive. Trust me. You're going to have a lot of fun,"
said Olive's dad. And just like that they were off to the city.

Olive and Oliver thought they had been driving forever. Then, off in the distance, they began to see a glow.

The closer they got, the more lights they saw. And there were signs everywhere. Olive tried to read the signs that were lit up, but her dad was driving too fast. Olive was in another world. Oliver, on the other hand, had earthly things on his mind. "I'm hungry," he said.

They finally reached the hotel and got out of the car. A large neon sign written in cursive caught Olive's attention.

"Red Tulip Hotel," Olive said aloud. "Is this our hotel? It's in the middle of everything. It doesn't look like the hotel we stayed at when we went to Game World."

"It is very different, Olive," said her dad, "but I promise you'll have a good time here, too."

Olive wasn't too sure. It was noisy. Cars were rushing by and honking. Lights were blinking on every street corner. Sirens were blaring.

The family checked in and the desk clerk gave them keys to a room on the seventh floor. They carried their bags to the elevator and then into their hotel room. Olive began to look for a television set. Oliver, however, wasn't interested in anything but food. "I'm starving," he whined.

"Okay, tourists, let's go find a restaurant," Olive's dad announced. "Let's walk this way."

"Walk?" Olive questioned. "Wouldn't it be faster to drive?"

"Not in the city," her mom said. "There are lots of sidewalks in the city. The city is a great place to walk. It's easier than taking the car and trying to find a parking spot. Some people take public transportation, but we're walking!"

"Whatever you say, Mom," Olive said in a way that told everyone she had her doubts.

Olive was starting to get cranky—seriously cranky. *Some surprise*, she thought. "A dog would have been a lot better surprise," she mumbled to herself.

Finally, the family stopped at a place called The Daisy Café. "My feet hurt," complained Olive.

"Yeah, mine too," added Oliver.

"Well, I heard this restaurant serves great meatloaf and mashed potatoes, so I hope you both are hungry," said Olive's mom.

Everyone ate until they were stuffed. "I like city food,"
Oliver announced.

As they walked back to the hotel, Olive tried to read every
sign and look at all the people. There was so much to look
at that she couldn't keep up with her mom and dad. She
had the most fun looking way up to the top of the huge
buildings they passed.

Everyone was yawning by the time they reached the hotel
room. They all went right to sleep, and before they knew it,
it was morning.

Is it morning already? Olive wondered. She opened her eyes, adjusted to the new surroundings, and thought: *Our first day in the city. This might be fun.*

Oliver was the first one to shower and dress. He couldn't wait to eat a "city breakfast." Olive's mom and dad had planned the day for them. They bought tickets to see a play in the afternoon. "What's a play?" Oliver asked his mother. Olive rolled her eyes. She already knew what a play was—it was like a TV show only with real people right in front of you. She was in no mood to hear a long explanation. She was in a hurry to get going. "Can I go down to the lobby and wait for you slowpokes?"

"Go ahead," said Olive's mom, "but please be careful. Make sure you stay in the lobby and don't wander off anywhere!"

Olive stepped into the elevator and pushed the "L" button for "lobby." She wouldn't admit it to anyone else, but she was feeling a little scared in there all by herself. Then the elevator stopped on the third floor.

The elevator doors opened and some people and LOTS of luggage piled into the elevator. Olive squished herself into the corner of the elevator to make room for all the luggage.

Finally, the elevator moved, and the doors opened again. Everyone piled out including Olive.

She looked out the huge front windows at what seemed to be a beautiful day outside. The sun was shining. She counted one, two, maybe three puffy white clouds. She saw the trees swaying and a woman passing by holding onto her hat. *It would be so funny if her hat flew away,* Olive thought as she smiled mischievously.

Olive watched the revolving door as people entered and exited the hotel. *I'm not supposed to leave the lobby,* she thought, *but no one said I couldn't walk through the revolving door. I'll still be in the lobby.*

So, she stepped inside the revolving door and started twirling.

No one was more surprised than Olive to find that she had twirled herself right out of the hotel and onto the city sidewalk. She was even more surprised to see six dogs that appeared out of nowhere. They were all sizes and colors, walking on leashes attached to one dog walker. Olive saw a tiny brown dog that looked like a hot dog, a puffy white one that looked like a big marshmallow, two big black dogs, one black and white dog, and one that was so tiny it could barely keep up with the other dogs.

"Cool," Olive said. *I'll just walk with them to the end of the block,* she thought. And that's what she did.

Olive followed the six dogs and their dog walker to the end of the block. And then she followed them around the corner, up the street, around another corner, through an alley, and back on another sidewalk.

That was fun, Olive thought, *but I'd better get back to the hotel.* Unfortunately, she had no idea where the hotel was.

Olive was usually pretty tough. She had no problem giving other kids at school a hard time. In fact, she had no problem giving her teachers a hard time. But now she had a big problem. She was lost in the city.

A lot of people passed by Olive, but she didn't know any of them. They were talking on phones or looking at papers or staring ahead blankly. They all looked too busy to talk to her. If the truth be told, Olive was beginning to feel a little scared.

Back in the hotel lobby, Olive's family was looking everywhere for her. Olive's dad talked to the clerk at the hotel registration desk. The clerk called the police station and said, "We have a missing girl. Can you send someone to help right away?"

Olive's dad started searching for Olive on the street. Olive's mom was crying. Oliver just held her hand.

"The streets of the city are no place for a little girl to be by herself," a voice called out to Olive. She looked up, tears welling in her eyes, and saw a police officer on a horse.

"Hi, young lady. My name is Officer Farber. Are you lost?"

"Yes," Olive replied in a voice that quivered more than Olive wanted it to.

"I think I can help you," Officer Farber said.

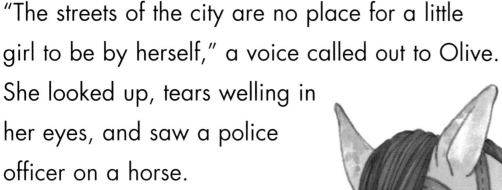

Olive told Officer Farber everything she could remember about her hotel. "It has a big cursive sign. Do you know what *cursive* means?" Olive asked. Officer Farber just smiled and nodded as he wrote notes on a pad of paper.

Olive continued, "Oh, it has a revolving door and it's close to a restaurant called The Daisy Café. And my dad's car is parked in the parking lot of the hotel." Officer Farber tied up his horse and took Olive's hand. Then the two of them started walking down the street.

The first hotel they passed was lovely, but it wasn't Olive's hotel. She looked up at Officer Farber, shook her head, and said, "Nope, this isn't it." So they kept walking. They stopped at the next hotel. This one had a big sign that said, "Indoor Pool." *That would be fun,* Olive thought, but then she shook her head and said, "Nope, that isn't our hotel."

Red Tulip Hotel

As Officer Farber and Olive continued down the street, Olive began to feel as if some things were looking familiar. Then she spotted the big neon sign. "This is it! This is it!" she squealed with joy.

Olive was starting to think that maybe she could have found her way back to the hotel by herself. She was hoping her family hadn't even gotten down to the lobby yet.

"Thanks, Officer Farber. This is my hotel. I'm fine now. Good-bye. Thank you," she said dismissively. But Officer Farber wasn't going anywhere. When they walked into the lobby, Olive spotted Oliver at the same moment he spotted her. Oliver yelled, "There's Olive with a policeman!"

Olive's mom ran across the room to Olive. She began hugging Olive and scolding her all at the same time. Olive's mom hugged Officer Farber, too.

"Mom, there were these dogs and …" Olive started to explain.

Officer Farber interrupted. He sounded a lot like Miss Millie as he talked about how dangerous it is to wander off alone. But Olive didn't roll her eyes. She listened and thought about what he said. Suddenly, Olive's dad rushed into the lobby. He hugged Olive and thanked Officer Farber.

"Are you a real police officer?" Oliver asked Officer Farber.

"I sure am, young man. You make sure to keep an eye on your sister from now on," he said. As Oliver seemed to puff up, Olive seemed to shrink.

As soon as Officer Farber left, Olive knew she had a lot of explaining to do.

"I know what I did was wrong," Olive began. "I think maybe we should glue my hand to yours so this never happens again!"

They all started to laugh as they headed out the revolving door. They were finally ready for a day in the city.